FRIED FEATHERS
FOR THANKSGIVING

by James Stevenson

 Greenwillow Books, New York

Watercolor paints were combined with pen drawings for the full-color illustrations.

First Edition   10 9 8 7 6 5 4 3 2 1

Library of Congress Cataloging-in-Publication Data
Stevenson, James, (date)   Fried feathers for Thanksgiving.
Summary: Mean witches Dolores and Lavinia try to spoil Thanksgiving
for everyone else but nice witch Emma and her friends outwit them.
[1. Witches—Fiction.   2. Thanksgiving—Fiction] I. Title.
PZ7.S84748Fr 1986   [E]   86-3100
ISBN 0-688-06675-5   ISBN 0-688-06676-3 (lib. ed.)